But Yesterday

A Play

Jimmie Chinn

A SAMUEL FRENCH ACTING EDITION

SAMUEL FRENCH

FOUNDED 1830

SAMUELFRENCH-LONDON.CO.UK
SAMUELFRENCH.COM

BUT YESTERDAY

First presented as a rehearsed reading by Teddington
Theatre Club, with the following cast:

Robert	Peter Slater
Howard	Jack Smeroon
Chloe	Cynthia Carss
Ruth	Freda Hammerton
The Woman	Jeanna Darnell

The play was directed by the **Author**

Characters

Robert
Howard
Chloe
Ruth
The Woman
Two men (non-speaking)

The play is set in part of a run-down garden at a vicarage

Time—the fifties and before

For Litti . . . with love and gratitude

BUT YESTERDAY

A garden, huge and rambling. A bench and a chair. The sounds of summer—but autumn is not far off. A feeling of expanse and desolation. An old vicarage lies unseen behind the trees

Music creeps in among the bird-song, melancholy and distant

The time is both now and then. The period—the fifties and before

Light filters through a cluster of trees

Robert enters the garden. He is dressed in a trilby hat, his jacket over his shoulder, a hand in his pocket

A light, brighter than the rest, comes up around him

He listens, his head on one side, almost bird-like

Robert This is the garden where I used to play . . . the swing . . . the tree I used to climb . . . the bird-bath—see—under the willow.

The music rises and falls

It was home . . . in what seemed like another age . . . another country almost. (*He looks into the middle distance*) And the gate—still held shut by a piece of string . . . there—beyond the lawn. It leads to Bishop's Wood and Tangle Hill . . . down to Jelly's Brook where we used to fish. (*He smiles, lost in the memory*) I remember falling in, one Sunday after church. Ruth slapped my legs and cried—she always cried—and Father said, "It doesn't matter . . ."

Distantly we hear an old steam train

And the sound of the old steam train as it chugged its way down to Hadcross, stopping at our station only on Mondays and Fridays—market days I suppose—and the fair, twice a year.

Ruth enters. She is unaware of Robert

Ruth (*calling off*) It seems cooler here. Slightly more shade.

Ruth stands quietly and looks about her, lost in thought, shading her eyes for the moment as she looks out into the distance—remembering

Robert Ruth was my aunt ... although I was never allowed to address her as such ...
Ruth (*distantly*) "Ruth—dear ..."
Robert She used to say ...
Ruth "I'm called Ruth—not Aunt ..." (*She sits on the bench and brushes away a fly*)
Robert She was my father's sister ... (*He goes to stand behind her*) She came to stay with us just after the war. A Sunday it was—it always seemed to be Sunday then. She wore a huge hat, I recall ... and white gloves. She stood in our drive as if reluctant to enter the house, as if she really belonged somewhere else, and although I didn't know it then she'd come to stay—for ever.

A woman's voice calls from a distance

Chloe (*off, distant, calling*) Ruth—look what we've found.
Ruth (*to herself*) Oh, how tiresome it all is. (*Aloud*) What, dear?
Chloe (*off, calling*) Ruth—I'm sure you're not listening.
Ruth (*to herself*) I shall go mad with it all. (*Aloud*) I *am* listening ... I am *really* listening ... (*To herself again*) The woman's a pest.
Robert Ruth never liked my mother all that much—nor my mother she. And yet they lived so closely—and for so long—under the same roof.

Chloe enters on the arm of Howard who appears at first to be blind and deaf. She wears a sun-hat, he a dog collar and a vicar's garb. Howard carries a stick and Chloe a canvas bag

Chloe (*as she enters*) Did you hear what we said?
Ruth I heard. The whole village heard. What is it?
Chloe (*always delighted by the trivial things in life*) Howard stumbled upon it—quite by chance.
Ruth Not a body—in the vicarage garden—whatever next I wonder ...
Chloe (*as if to a child*) Not a body, Ruth. We mustn't be silly must we, dear? Howard—tell her—tell Ruthie what we've chanced upon—after all these years.

*Chloe is hiding something behind her back. Ruth hasn't even turned
to look*

Howard (*through blind eyes, trying to get his bearings*) Where n
the world are we? Do I know this place?
Chloe (*having had years of this behaviour*) Of course you know this
place, Howard—don't get out of hand, dear.
Howard Am I being abducted? Shall I be held to ransom?
Chloe (*sitting him in a chair*) We're at home—safe and sound—as
usual. This is our garden.
Howard I know all that—I mean where are we *exactly*?
Chloe We crossed the upper lawn—we turned left at the rhodo-
dendrons—straight on past the gloxinia—through the old vege-
table patch and by the tennis nets—and we're here—by the
willow and the swing. (*She sits beside Ruth on the bench*) As
Ruthie said, it's cooler here—not so stifling.
Howard Were there young folk? Playing tennis? Did I hear the
sound of bat against ball?
Chloe (*humouring him as always*) Of course, dear. They come for
miles to play on our court. Charábancs arrive every hour. We
shall have to start making tea for them, sevenpence a cup.
Ruthie here could make brandy snaps. We could make ourselves
useful—no?

No reply. They fall silent

Robert (*moving away down stage*) These were my parents. They
had long since packed up and left the real world. Circumstances
had caused them to invent a different existence—a safer one.
They never spoke of intimate things—of worldly matters. Such
things were a threat to the thin shell of fantasy with which they
had surrounded themselves. Father, on a day in the late fifties,
had decided to feign deafness. It was easier than having to listen
to Ruth and my mother all day long. It wasn't until much later
that he decided to go "blind" as well.
Howard Shall I paint my stick white, I wonder. Might people not
suspect I am afflicted thus?
Chloe I am your white stick, Howard, just as I'm your hearing-
aid, your invalid-chair, and your nurse-maid. We haven't the
money to waste on a cripple's accoutrements. (*She brushes a fy
away*) It's so long since we were down here—the flies think it's
their birthday.

They fall silent. There is only the sound of the birds

Robert Nothing touched us here. Time passed un-noticed—days were endless. It never rained, seldom did you hear the wind. Once a year the cuckoo paid its visit. The kingfisher. And occasionally the fox. But none of them seemed to want to stay. The garden belonged only to us—Mother, Father ... Ruth. I can't ever remember a stranger here. (*Pause. He recalls*) Except them, but that was later.

Chloe You still haven't asked what Howard and I discovered on our travels, Ruthie.

Ruth How remiss of me, Chloe. I'm sure you're going to tell me.

Chloe This, dear. (*She produces a small rubber ball*) Imagine. After all these years. Robert's ball—you remember.

Ruth (*looking at it, the past rushing towards her*) Yes ... as you say ... after all this time.

Chloe (*putting it into her canvas bag*) I'm going to tuck it away. Just imagine his surprise to have it restored to him.

Ruth (*almost to herself*) How the mind plays tricks. I'd convinced myself it was red—and yet it appears to be a dingy yellow.

Chloe It's taken on the colour of its hiding place—it's lain there so long.

Ruth It seems but yesterday that it vanished—

Chloe (*not listening, pointing, excited*) Oh, look—quick—there's Mr Squirrel!

Howard Where?

Chloe You can't see—remember.

Howard You'll have to describe him to me.

Chloe I have better things to do with my time. It'll soon be tea— more skivvying—boiling kettles, buttering bread, washing up. Life's tedious routine.

Ruth We could always do without. We shan't starve. I think we eat far too much.

Chloe Your brother here is on his last legs. The doctor recommends a regular diet. Who'll take the blame if he dies?

Ruth He won't die—at least not before us he won't. He's at a distinct advantage—aren't you, Howard? You have the Almighty on your side.

Robert Whole days were spent listening to Ruth and my mother bickering. Occasionally a bus would pass on its way to the City. You could just see it through the trees. It would stop by the post

office to pick up Mr Roach who was the only person in our
village who ever seemed to go anywhere. He had a special pass
long before such things were thought of, and it enabled him to
come and go as he pleased. All this was a constant source of
speculation and gossip to my mother.

Chloe I'm sure Mr Roach has murdered his wife.

Ruth I do hope so—something must happen soon.

Chloe It's my belief he's cut her into little pieces. Have you noticed
those sordid little carrier bags of his? Mark my words—*she's* in
there—a different bit every day. He catches that bus and dumps
her over bridges onto passing trains. Are you listening, Howard?

Howard You seem to forget. I'm deaf. Besides—I thought we
buried Mrs Roach many years back.

Ruth Trust you, Howard, to spoil everything.

*The music returns, just below the sound of the birds. Robert removes
his hat and sits on the ground. All four seem to hold their faces to the
sunshine, each lost in their own thoughts*

(*Suddenly, calling across time and distance, as if to a child*)
Robert—come back here at once—you mustn't go through the
gate!

Howard (*also in the past*) Leave him, Ruth—leave him to wander.

Ruth (*standing and looking into the distance, fear in her voice*) He
mustn't go beyond the gate . . . he's not allowed to go into the
wood, Howard.

Chloe (*amused by Ruth's concern*) The more you tell him not to
go—the more he'll want to.

Ruth You stupid woman—can't you see he might get lost—hurt
even.

Howard (*embarrassed by her attitude to Chloe*) Ruth.

Chloe Leave her, Howard. (*To Ruth*) Howard and I *are* the child's
parents, Ruth. We are capable of doing our duty.

Ruth Then do it. Call him. (*She calls loudly*) Robert!

Howard (*standing*) Robert—come back here.

Robert (*looking in the same direction as them*) I heard them, I
heard them calling. But I opened the gate and went anyway. It
gave me a feeling of power to know I could cause such friction
between them.

Chloe It's Bishop's Wood, for heaven's sake, not the Amazon
Jungle. He'll be back when it's tea-time.

Ruth turns and looks at Chloe then goes to stand a little way off, her back to them. We can see she is upset

Robert It wasn't until years later that I discovered what a house of strangers I had been brought up in. Father with his religion, Mother trying so hard to be a perfect vicar's wife. And Ruth. Ruth, lost—and with such sadness in her eyes. Each of them in desperate need of the other—but unable to admit it. Nothing was ever said—but it hung in the air like a haunting piece of music that reverberated above the trees . . .

Chloe (*rising*) I suppose I'd better go and fetch him . . . as if I hadn't enough to do.

Chloe exits DL

Silence. The music has faded again. Howard sits

Howard (*quietly to Ruth and without turning back*) You really must try to control these—outbursts.

Ruth (*also quietly, calmer now*) It seems I'm not even allowed to care about the boy.

Howard You are, Ruth. Of course you are. But in moderation.

Ruth As you know, I'm unfamiliar with moderation. I don't know what it means.

Howard (*as if referring to another subject*) Yes . . . well.

Silence. Ruth sits again

(*as if it had waited long enough to be said*) Chloe and I . . . we feel . . .

Ruth What?

Howard We think that perhaps it's time the boy went away.

Ruth Away?

Howard To school. We feel the change could only do him good. We lead such a cloistered life here at the vicarage . . . we feel he should be mixing more . . . with boys his own age. Life here has a habit of passing us by.

Ruth gives a cry, almost one of laughter

I'm sure you'll agree with our decision. I had intended to tell you, sooner or later.

Ruth So—it *is* a decision then? You *have* decided.

Howard As of this moment—yes. I had promised Chloe I would think about it—I have—and I've reached the conclusion that I'm all in favour. The time has come for change. Come next autumn the boy shall pack his bags and journey forth to Cirencester.

Ruth Cirencester—never heard of it!

Howard Now you're being obtuse, Ruth. Of course you've heard of Cirencester—everyone in the world has heard of Cirencester. Glos.

Ruth And *she* approves of this, does she?

Howard If, by *she*, you mean Chloe—yes, she does.

Ruth The boy is ten, Howard—ten years old. What mother worthy of the title would pack a boy of ten off to some God-forsaken boarding school in Gloucestershire?

Howard Hardly God-forsaken—the school is attached to one of the finest theological colleges in England.

Ruth My God, you're turning the child into a bible thumper before puberty! Mother always said you were a demon at heart.

Howard You can insult me all you wish, Ruth . . . the dye is cast.

Ruth That woman has made a monster of you, Howard. I pity you.

Howard Save any pity for yourself, Ruth. In time you may need it. Robert is our responsibility. And that is final.

Howard and Ruth fall silent

Robert I was never sure what they spoke of when I was not there. I only knew there were "grown-up" conversations, hushed voices behind half-closed doors, abrupt endings as I entered a room. Remarks such as "shh, not in front of the boy!" "Run along, Robert, go and play in the garden".

We hear an old steam train in the distance

(*Smiling, happy*) There it goes . . . the old steam train to Hadcross.

Chloe returns, hands behind her back and whistling, in the present once more. She stops in her tracks and looks back

Howard (*"blind" again*) Are you back?

Chloe (*without turning to him*) You know very well I'm back.

Howard Yes.

Chloe Then why bother to ask? I've been for a saunter—a jaunt—
you see the most amazing sights. Did you know most of our
fence is down?

Howard Really?

Chloe Blown clean away.

Howard The wind, I expect.

Chloe Even the bit that's left has been defiled—posters. Stuck
there by those wretched operatic creatures. Though who they
expect to see them stuck on our back fence is beyond me.

Howard I hear they're doing *The Mikado* again.

Chloe I shouldn't wonder—"doing" being the operative word.
Poor old G and S have a lot to answer for.

Howard We have to go—it's our duty.

Silence. Chloe turns and walks up stage

Chloe I dare say you've been talking about me.

Chloe goes to stand further off—alone

Robert Even though on occasions I would slip un-noticed into
Bishop's Wood—or climb up to the top of Tangle Hill—Ruth
was never far away.

*Ruth rises and stands just behind Robert. She shades her eyes and
looks out into the distance*

Wherever I went—I could sense her presence—and it was never
long before I would hear her voice.

Ruth (*calling*) Robert ...

Robert From my earliest recollections it was always she who was
there ... at bed-time to put me to bed ... in the morning to wake
me ... at bath-time ... (*He seems sad and lost*) It was even she
who told me what, in a way, I'd always suspected. I was home
for the summer holidays and, as usual, sitting out here ...

Ruth (*looking down at him*) You seem miles away.

Robert No, not really, I was just thinking.

Ruth (*gently*) What about?

Robert Being old ... of being old and living here ... spending
whole days like this ... with nothing to do and nowhere
to go ...

Ruth sits down just behind him

Ruth You're far too young to be thinking such things ...

Robert When I'm away I never do. But here, on days like these, I often wonder what it'll be like.

Chloe speaks in the present, unlike Ruth and Robert who are in the past

Chloe We should come out here more often. (*She sits on the bench*)
Howard (*through blind eyes*) Did you speak?
Chloe Bring a picnic. Spread a cloth upon the ground . . . set with china cups and plates . . . fish-paste sandwiches . . . scones with honey . . . flasks of tea.
Howard Too late. It was different when the boy was here. Then there was a reason.

Howard and Chloe fall silent

Robert Ruth? Do you think they'll be disappointed if I don't go into the church?
Ruth I'm sure they'll be furious—but I shouldn't let it worry you.
Robert Perhaps it would be best to say nothing. Just yet anyway.
Ruth The moment will present itself—it usually does.
Robert I'm not sure I believe in . . . all that.
Ruth Shhh—the trees have ears—they may tell on you. You must learn to be secretive—like me.

Robert looks at her

There are things we wouldn't want them to know.

A silence hovers

Robert Why am I not like them?
Ruth Would you want to be?
Robert I've tried—every day of my life I try to be like them. But somehow—it's difficult. I look at them—watch them—eating—talking—going about their business. I sit in church listening to his sermons. I look across at him—up there in the pulpit—at the altar praying—and I don't know who he is. Is that wrong do you think?
Ruth It's not so strange.
Robert I've never told anyone this, but at school I used to imagine my parents coming to see me—you know—on open days. I'd sit at my window looking down on the drive as all the other parents arrived in their cars. I'd search among the faces—but my

parents were never there. I'd wait to be told—yet again—that Father was unwell—or that Mother had a headache. But then I'd see them. "They *have* turned up" I thought . . . But then—I'd look more closely. They *were* my parents—I knew that. But they weren't Howard and Chloe at all—they were strangers.

Silence. A distant train whistle blows. The birds sing

Ruth I hate them both.
Robert Oh, now . . .
Ruth I do. I can't help it. I loathe them.
Robert (*uncomfortable now, attempting to rise*) Perhaps we've said enough . . .
Ruth (*restraining him*) Too late. I said the moment usually presents itself—you have to know sooner or later. If they had any sense they'd have told you years ago.

There is no reply from Robert. He waits

Howard (*almost breaking the mood*) Is it chilly out here? Are there clouds? In the sky?

There is no answer

Are you there?
Chloe (*deep in thought*) I've seen the way she looks at him. It's unnatural. History has a habit of repeating itself, Howard. We must send her away from here.

Ruth rises, almost girlishly, and wanders upstage, her back to us. Robert, having heard dreadful news, just stares out in front of him

Howard I can't do that. I promised to look after her. I can't send her away.
Robert (*calling, almost an echo*) Ruth . . . ?
Chloe Then *he* must go. It isn't a perfect world. We can't have everything.

The music rises

There is a shift in emphasis in the lighting

  A Young Woman enters the garden

Howard, Chloe and Ruth turn to see the Woman. Robert remains silent, downstage, still staring out

Chloe (*to the Woman*) But why so modest? Come—come and join us. It's not often we see a new face.

The Woman comes forward shyly

Woman Forgive me—I was told this was the vicarage.
Chloe It is. And my husband, here, the vicar.
Woman I'm exhausted. I took a train in London, then a bus to here. It dropped me by the post office. I asked a child—and here I am.
Chloe You make it sound like an adventure. I'm afraid we never leave the village, we lead rather a dull life.

Ruth is looking on as if she knows the Woman

Howard (*puzzled by a stranger*) Chloe?
Chloe You must forgive my husband—his sight you know. Don't stand so far off—come—over here—where the sun is brightest.

The Woman comes further down stage into a pool of light

Woman (*looking about*) And you must be Ruth—he spoke of you often.
Chloe (*a little too sharply*) He?
Woman You are Robert's parents?
Chloe (*pleased*) We are. He sent you? Have you news of him?
Woman No. I came hoping that you had. I thought perhaps—a letter?
Howard Our son prefers to keep us in the dark. We are the last to be told anything.
Woman (*obviously disappointed*) Oh dear. (*Lightheaded*) I'm sorry, may I? (*She indicates a seat*)
Chloe Please—Please do. You seem unwell—can I . . . ?
Woman I shall be fine—if I could sit for a moment. (*She sits*)
Chloe Our son is in foreign parts. We received a phone call from him, oh, several months ago. He said he was off to—where, Howard?
Howard Humm?
Chloe (*ignoring him*) To somewhere far distant. We never travel, er, Miss. We wouldn't know one place from another. You know him? You're friends?
Woman (*quietly*) Yes. I know him.

Howard rises and turns a little way upstage. Ruth has not moved, she simply looks on. Chloe, as usual, is aware of an atmosphere but is only confused

Chloe Howard—don't wander off. (*To the Woman*) I could make lemonade, that might refresh you . . . ?
Woman That would be nice, if it's no trouble.
Chloe Of course. And perhaps Ruth will show you the garden. (*She lowers her voice*) And I think my husband has need of the lavatory. (*She goes up to Howard and takes his arm*) Come along, dear, you've only to ask.

Chloe and Howard exit

Ruth, left alone with the Woman, looks on from behind

The music is heard softly

Robert (*to us*) It wasn't until later that I discovered *she* had been here. Even then, it was Ruth who told me. If ever my parents had any doubt that we had grown apart *her* visit confirmed it.
Woman (*quietly to Ruth*) You, I'm sure, know who I am.
Ruth (*quietly*) Yes. I know.
Woman Robert told *you*, then?
Ruth (*coming downstage to beside the Woman*) No. He doesn't have to tell *me* anything. We think alike—he and I.
Woman I see.
Ruth You knew him at Cambridge?
Woman (*half to Ruth, half to herself*) Yes. We met quite by chance, in a park just outside the city. I used to go there to eat my lunch. There was a little stream and a footbridge, and a signpost which said "To the tea rooms". But there weren't any tea rooms—they'd been vandalized and left unused. And there was a paddling pool . . . but it had no water. Winter and summer alike—it had no water. And one day I saw him. He was lying on the grass reading a book—"Conquest of Minds" it was called. It had a blue cover—blue—with an elastic band which he placed in the page when he'd finished reading. And at once I knew he was different. The way he lay there, with no interest in being noticed. But he waved as I passed, as if he knew me—as if he'd seen me before. And yet I know I'd never seen him. Somewhere— unseen—children were playing in the park, you could hear them, laughing.

Ruth (*unhappy that Robert is being spoken of thus*) You're not as I
imagined . . .

Woman (*not hearing this perhaps*) We were immediately comfor-
table together. I sat beside him on the lawns, and although we
must have spoken I can't remember what he said. We saw each
other again, the next afternoon, and the next, and each time we
talked and talked but I can't remember the conversations.
Except—he always mentioned Russia—and his love of it—and
his desire, one day, to visit there. Often we didn't speak at all,
but it never felt wrong. We would simply look across at each
other and he'd smile, the way he sometimes does, you know.

Ruth smiles to herself—she understands

And on our wedding day we smiled at each other in just that
same way. Nothing was said. Not "I love you"! Not "I need
you" . . . just a look that meant—"I'm glad you're there" . . .

Ruth (*perhaps to break the tenderness in the Woman's voice*) And
now he's gone . . . left you, you think?

Woman No. No—he wouldn't do that. He's careless that's all,
thoughtless. It wouldn't cross his mind that I might be worried.

Ruth He learned to be self-sufficient here, in this garden. He
learned never to be dependent on anyone. It's best for all
concerned. (*Pause*) I'm sorry you've come all this way for
nothing.

Woman (*looking at Ruth now*) You know him better than anyone,
he told me that. May I confide in you—please?

Ruth I feel I must warn you—I'm past being burdened with other
people's worries. We have our own—here.

Woman I've no one else, Ruth.

Ruth What about your family—what about them?

Woman They don't know about Robert. It seemed to give him
pleasure to keep our marriage a secret. At first—it was like a
childish game—and I, too, enjoyed the idea of being mysterious.
But now, it's backfired on me. When I need my parents' help I'm
unable to ask for it. Like Robert—I never even wrote to them.

Ruth I see.

Woman I'd have to tell them, you see—I'd have to tell them who
he is. (*Pause*) You've read the newspapers I suppose.

Ruth We never take a newspaper—but when you live in a village—people tend to gossip. I gather he's famous—quite suddenly?

Woman Infamous—surely? Do *they* know?

Ruth I'm not sure. We only concern ourselves with trivial matters here. We gave up speaking the truth many years ago.

Woman But he's their son.

Ruth Robert plays no part in their lives now—he belongs to yesterday—and yesterday is seldom touched upon in this house.

Woman Then what am I to do?

Ruth I'm afraid you've come to the wrong place if you expect help from my brother and his wife—they said goodbye to Robert when he was ten years old.

Woman He never comes back here then?

Ruth Oh yes, occasionally. But only to wander in the garden, the woods. He goes for walks.

Woman If . . . if he turns up—could you tell him that I called—that I'd like to hear from him.

Ruth *If* he turns up . . . and if I feel he *needs* to be told . . . then yes—I shall mention your visit.

Woman Thank you.

Silence. The Woman seems more relaxed, she breathes in the fresh air

It's nice here—peaceful.

Ruth I can appreciate, that to a stranger, it might appear so.

Woman Perhaps I should go now?

Ruth My sister-in-law is fetching lemonade—she might be disappointed.

Woman Of course.

Ruth We have other things to drink—more effective than lemonade. But they're locked away.

Chloe returns, a glass of lemonade in her hand

Chloe (*cheerfully*) To quench the thirst . . . and revive the spirits.

Ruth turns away and moves upstage. The Woman takes the glass and drinks

Chloe It's not out of a bottle. We hate those gassy concoctions. I take a lemon—squeeze it—add a small amount of sugar—some cool, clear water—and hey presto!

Woman It's good. Thank you.

Howard appears anxiously in the shadows at the back

Chloe (*lowering her voice*) I do hope Ruth hasn't been troubling you with her nonsense, she does tend to be full of her own importance, and my husband . . . he . . .

Howard (*calling over*) Chloe? Did you ask the young lady?

Chloe (*urgently*) He worries far too much. Like his sister, he imagines things. You must just ignore them.

Howard (*calling*) Is she who we think?

Chloe (*nervous, afraid, close to tears*) You can see for yourself the kind of life we lead. You shouldn't have come. The fabric here is very delicate—visitors from the outside world can break it.

Woman (*understanding Chloe's intentions*) I was about to leave. I'm sorry if I've caused a fuss.

Howard (*anxiously*) Chloe? Are you there?

Chloe He'll be like this till bedtime. Shall I take your glass? (*She does so*) I'm sorry we cannot be of help. If things had been different . . .

Woman I'm sorry too, I would like to have known you.

Chloe (*after a pause, unable to say anything more*) Yes. (*She turns and goes back to Howard. Quietly, as she exits*) Come along, dear. Best indoors.

Howard (*as he exits on Chloe's arms*) Did you ask? Did you enquire?

Chloe and Howard have gone

The Woman stands quietly. She looks out into the distance

Ruth I'm not fond of my sister-in-law, but she, too, knows the awfulness of being alive.

Silence

Woman (*looking out*) I see everything clearly now. I'm glad I came—he's to blame for all this.

Ruth (*rather than protest*) I'd like it if you left now, please. There's a gate at the end. It'll save you going through the house.

Silence. The Woman doesn't move

Robert I never saw my wife again. But I think of her . . . in the evenings mostly . . . or lying alone on my bed. I thought—on those sunny afternoons in the park—she was the one thing I had ever wanted. But I was wrong. If it was love I was searching for—she taught me that I would never find it in a person, but—in a *place*, far, far distant.

The Woman walks slowly away—down left and off

The music rises

The lighting changes

We are in the present again

Chloe is heard off, singing. She enters, arm-in-arm with Howard. They are laughing and happy

Chloe (*singing*)	"It's a long way to Tipperary, It's a long way to go …
Howard (*singing*)	"Without your mother …
Chloe (*singing*)	"It's a long way to Tipperary, To the sweetest girl I know …"

Howard Where the hell are we?

Chloe Oh, don't start all that again. We're here—back where we started. See—Ruthie's here, waiting for us.

Ruth, not amused by their silly games, sits again

Chloe (*to Ruth*) Did you catch sight of Mr Fox?

Ruth Sadly—I missed him.

Chloe Oh, such a pity, Ruthie, he looked magnificent in the sunshine. But I'm afraid we scared him off with our singing.

Chloe helps Howard to sit in his chair

Howard (*happily*) I've had the most wonderful idea. Perhaps tomorrow, we could go out.

Ruth Here we go.

Howard We could take the car, travel to the seaside, buy chips in newspaper and eat them on the sands. Do as other folks do. No? We've no ties—nothing to prevent us.

Ruth (*tired of it all*) You said that yesterday, and the day before.

Chloe (*sitting beside Ruth*) Let him say it, Ruthie, it passes the time.

Ruth He should be stopped—that way madness lies.

Chloe So—he's mad. I'm mad, you're mad, we're all mad! I talk to the coal-skuttle—the sideboard—even the chain on the lavatory. If we kept a cat I'd talk to that. Personally, I don't think it *is* madness. Those who don't talk at all—they're the mad ones. Do you agree, Howard?

She looks over at him. No reply. Silence

Howard (*for the sake of something to say*) What's for supper?
Chloe Carrots.
Howard Carrots. Is that all? No meat?
Chloe We can't have meat *all* the time. You'll have carrots and like it. "These carrots are Spanish!", I said to the woman in the shop. "Is nothing English any more?" She refused to comment—sullen bitch. I'm sure she's done away with her husband—you never see him.

They fall silent

The Lights fade leaving Howard, Chloe and Ruth staring into space—lost in their own thoughts

A pool of light comes up on Robert. He rises and starts to put on his jacket for the first time. And his hat and a pair of wire spectacles. He looks different now—older perhaps and more severe

Robert I made the journey by car that day. The first time I hadn't used the train or the bus. *They* wanted to see where I was born. And I—I wanted one last look at the garden—Bishop's Wood— and Tangle Hill. The news had broken. They said it was time to make a move. I'd helped them all I could but the other two had lost their nerve and told. Now, they said, I could be of more use over there. "You'll not miss it," they said. "You're one of us now, anyway." I saw the old steam train, chugging its way cross country. Today was Monday—today it would stop at my station. But we sped past. We overtook it by the bridge at Hadcross. *They* didn't notice but there was a boy at one of the windows. He was looking out as if this was his first journey by train. A small boy—his face aglow with excitement. He saw me—he waved.

The sound of an old steam train is heard

Two Men, in overcoats and hats, enter the garden. They stand upstage, part in shadow and in profile. They never move

The Lights come up again slowly on the garden. The single light on Robert fades

Howard, Chloe and Ruth turn to Robert

Howard (*no longer "blind"*) But why such haste? Tell us more. And why no letter for so long?
Chloe Questions, questions, Howard—you'll frighten the young man off. And who are your friends?
Robert (*avoiding the question*) And Ruth—you look so well. (*He goes to Ruth and puts an arm around her*) Oh, it's good to be back. See—everything's just as I remember it.
Ruth Are you happy?
Robert I'm happy, because there's so much to do, Ruth.
Ruth I'm glad.
Chloe At least allow me to make tea for you and your chums.
Robert Really, Mother, it *is* kind of you ... but we can't stay.
Howard At least tell us about the job—or is that a secret too?
Chloe All those foreign places—and look at us—we never move from this spot.
Robert How is the village?
Ruth As sleepy as ever—you're not missing a thing.
Howard Except us, Ruthie, except us, please. (*Lowering his voice a little*) Robert—this is more than a little awkward. (*He indicates the strangers*) Will you not introduce these gentlemen?
Robert Really, Father, they speak so few words of English ...
Chloe Italians, I'm sure—from your visit.
Robert (*not speaking the truth*) Yes—yes, Italians.

There is an awkward silence. Robert, uneasy now, moves away from them

Mother, Father ... Ruth—(*it is not easy to say*)
Ruth (*knowing by instinct*) You're going away.
Robert Well ...
Chloe What's so new in that? Paris, Berlin, Washington. He belongs to The Foreign Office now ... or British Intelligence ... which is it?

There is no reply. Howard, lost, sits down again and turns his head away. Ruth looks on. Robert is uncomfortable. Chloe is bewildered. We see, perhaps for the first time, her vulnerability

I realize I'm not quick to catch on—but what is wrong here?

Robert Nothing's *wrong*, Mother.

Chloe (*forcefully*) Liar!

Howard (*upset, but quietly*) Chloe, shh, now, shh.

Chloe (*her fear and anger unleashed*) I suppose Ruth is in on everything. You've always preferred to tell *her* your little secrets. We *are* your parents, young man, we have a right to know what you're up to! (*She looks about helplessly for support*) That's right—isn't it?

Robert (*looking directly at Chloe*) But you're not, are you?

Chloe (*hurt, indignant*) I beg your pardon.

Ruth (*to save any more hurt*) He knows, Chloe, for God's sake—he knows. Leave it now.

Howard is weeping softly

Chloe (*lost now*) We treated you as our son, we fed you, kept you safe. We loved you.

Robert Mother—how can you speak of love—you, who has lived without love all these years.

Chloe (*rising*) How dare you, how dare you come here, young man, and speak of things you know nothing about?

Howard Chloe . . .

Chloe They whisper about us because of you. They stay away from your father's church. They even cross the road when they see us . . .

Robert (*loudly*) If we had spoken the truth . . .

Chloe (*in a rage*) "Communist!", they whisper . . . "Communist " I've heard it. Don't stop me now—this pretence has gone on for too long!

Robert Yes, it has, from the day you brought me here. All our lives.

Chloe (*shouting now*) Leave us! Get away from here—and take these silent friends of yours. A vicarage garden is no place for a traitor!

The word is spoken. A sound seems to reverberate around the garden

Chloe stares at Robert for a moment—then, quietly she turns and walks away. She exits

Silence

Robert sees his father's distress

Howard (*rising, bewildered, quietly*) I must go to her ...
Robert Father ...
Howard She needs me ... I must go to my wife ...

Howard slowly walks off. He exits

Silence. After a moment, Ruth starts to laugh, quietly at first, but then the laughter begins to rise. Robert doesn't look at her—he stares out into space

Ruth (*pulling herself together*) Oh dear, I am sorry, I shouldn't really laugh. Your comrades, by the look of them, aren't used to it. I hope they won't shoot me. (*Pause*) It's strange. I never thought of you as a fool. (*Pause*) Walking in here, forcing to the surface what has been quite happily simmering beneath it for so long. (*Pause*) What, I wonder, did you hope to achieve?
Robert I'm a vicar's son—I was taught politeness. I felt it only polite to come and say goodbye.
Ruth Rather sentimental I would have thought—considering the circumstances. You'll be saying you're sorry next.
Robert No. I believed in what I did. But it's no use trying to make you understand that—your knowledge of anything beyond this garden is non-existent.
Ruth Ahh. There speaks the voice of experience.
Robert I'm sorry, Ruth—that was harsh of me.

Silence

Ruth Why *did* you come back?
Robert The garden, perhaps—the woods—you.
Ruth That pleases me ... and yet I'm surprised to find that I feel uncomfortable.
Robert Why? Because of them? (*He indicates the two strangers*)
Ruth No—they make no difference. Maybe, knowing nothing definite about you I was able to sketch in imaginary details— details more suited to my idea of you. I suppose that's one of my faults ... I refuse to see what is actually there.
Robert That's what this place does for you—here everything's only an illusion—imaginary.
Ruth Perhaps we like it that way and I've only just realized it. Our experiences of the real world have never been pleasant.

Pause

This place you're going to—this Utopia—what do you expect to find there?

Robert Honesty, a place where they speak the truth, where nothing's hidden. I've played your game for too long, Ruth.

Silence. Ruth moves away, her back to him

Who are you? What is your past?

Silence

Ruth (*her back to him*) I'm your aunt. And my past is of no consequence—now.

Robert Howard and Chloe, they know, but they never say.

Ruth Whatever their frailties—Howard and Chloe are loyal (*Pause*) Unlike you, they never betray secrets.

Silence

Robert It's time. (*He goes to the two strangers in the shadows*)

Ruth comes down stage, away from them

Ruth By the way, she came.

Robert (*between the two men, turning*) She?

Ruth The woman. She was asking after you. I'll write, I'll drop her a line. I'll tell her you never came back. Lying is often the simpler way out.

The music creeps in

Robert turns and walks away with the two Men. They exit

The music rises. The Lights slowly fade

The Play is over

FURNITURE AND PROPERTY LIST

On stage:	Bench Chair Other dressing as desired
Off-stage:	Glass of lemonade **(Chloe)**
Personal:	**Howard:** stick **Chloe:** canvas bag, small rubber ball **Robert:** pair of wire spectacles

LIGHTING PLOT

One exterior setting. A garden. Late summer

To open: Light filtering through trees

Cue 1	**As Robert enters** *Light comes up on Robert*	(Page 1)
Cue 2	Music rises *Shift in emphasis in lighting*	(Page 13)
Cue 3	Music rises *Lighting change*	(Page 16)
Cue 4	They fall silent *Lights fade. Pool of light comes up on Robert*	(Page 17)
Cue 5	Steam train is heard *Lights up on garden. Pool of light on Robert fades*	(Page 17)
Cue 6	Music rises *Lights slowly fade to black-out*	(Page 21)

EFFECTS PLOT

MADE AND PRINTED IN GREAT BRITAIN BY
LATIMER TREND & COMPANY LTD PLYMOUTH

MADE IN ENGLAND